FEELS LIKE YOU

CHARULATA

Made with ♥ on the Notion Press Platform
www.notionpress.com

For those who survived the storms and chose to live.

Contents

Contents

Contents

Contents

Contents

Foreword

Be ready to feel love, hate, pain.

Preface

Dear readers,

Thank you for chosing this book! thank you for spending your money and time to read my book.

your love is the reason i am still pursuing writing.

love,

charu

Acknowledgements

(மாற்றம் ஒன்றே மாறாதது)

Change is the only constant

Prologue

Love is a feeling that cannot be defined by any language, everyone here deserves to be loved hopelessly by someone. Sometimes love isn't enough, it needs compatibility, humility and commitment to gro. Love can't stand on its own and love does not always equal happily ever after. A part of me will always be searching for the piece of puzzle.

Everything has an opposite which can't exist with one another. Like the dark and the light. Without each other, we never know its value. Likewise we never know the value of someone until we lose them.

The love I gave
Is the love I saved.

Pre[illegible]

[illegible] deserves to be loved hopelessly by someone. Someone who [illegible] enough [illegible] needs [illegible] humility and [illegible] stand on its own [illegible] not always equal [illegible] always [illegible] for the perfect [illegible].

[illegible] the dark, [illegible]

[illegible]

[illegible]

Chapter1

The people who celebrate our birth
The people who validate our presence
Throughout the journey of life, family is constant
Mother is always mother
Father is always father.
Family is the boomerang of our life
The farther you keep them,
They always find a way back to us.

Chapter2

It was my first day,
I held my father's shirt with my tiny fingers
A kerchief pinned on my dress
With oily hair, tears in my eyes
I stood in front of the big building
Hoping I would go back home soon.
My father waved his hand
I started to cry.

Chapter3

After the exhausting day in school
My uncle picked me up,
I was hungry, I had nothing but water
There was a small bakery,
It had cookies, cakes, buns and sandwiches
Something about the bun caught my eyes '
Hot buns, abundance of jam and cream
Packed in a transparent cover,
My stomach started to growl
He noticed my love for the bun
He bought two buns,
I couldn't hold it with my small hands
Yet a smile bloom in my face and heart.

Chapter4

We both were alone,
With our lunch box filled
But none by our side.
You smiled, I smiled back
You looked at me with tears in your eyes'
I stood up, sat by your side
And I still do.

Chapter5

We bought one KitKat, split into four
That's when our bond started,
Sharing our chocolate, sharing our days
With days the bond grew
More than ever.

Chapter6

I miss those days where math was the only problem,
I miss those days where the only chemistry between me and hydrochloric acid,
That's the only chemistry that worked out.
I miss those days where my only worry was to save my lunch,
I miss those days where I bunked with my friends,
And say in the corner of our labs
I miss those boring lectures where I slept
I miss the love & care.

Chapter7

We giggled and caught our teacher's attention
"GET OUT" she shouted
We stood out, watching the people in our corridor.
Isn't she pretty?
Isn't he handsome?
We talked about random people walking by
We played XO in my rough note
We put flames with our crush name.
That's when we became friends,
And we still are the same kid in our heart.

Chapter8

It was three in the afternoon
We had our boards tomorrow
No one could concentrate
We started to talk, a simple conference call
Bound to be the blossom of new bond
The everlasting friendship filled with,
Love, care, affection and protection
Till now the one call is the most needed
To mend my soul.

Chapter9

I bought my first notebook
Spiral binding, white paper
Spiderman picture, with cool background
Like a small kid, I got excited to write in it
I wrote my name. Turned to the next page
I put the note on my face,
To get the smell of fresh pages
I started to write about my pain and gain
(The beginning of an era)

Chapter10

I picked up a book,
I held it in my hand
I started to read
I fell in love with the words
I could never get over it,
It was a companion at late night
I got fictional boyfriends over time
I fell in love with many
But didn't get my heart broken
To the books that saved me,
(Thank you)

Chapter11

The fluffy little cat,
With those cute little eyes
Looked me in the eyes, with it's sad "meow meow"
I gave some milk, I spent some time
I touched his forehead for the first time
It was soft, like a little baby
That's the first encounter of the,
Love of my life.

Chapter12

I was always left out
Other kids played without me
They hung out without me
They started to make fun of me
I was different from them
I didn't talk back
I didn't stand up for myself
Instead i cried alone
I still do.

Chapter13

(First crush)

He was wearing a mixed color shirt with white stripes,
Red sneakers, messy hair, four eyes
Little nerdy but lowkey cute
He caught my eye with his smile
Those moments when our eyes met in the corridor,
Blood rushed through my heart
Making it beat faster
I wrote his name in desk
When I visit my school
I could still see his name embedded in the desk
Till now he makes my heart flutter.

Chapter14

I entered into this world
To escape the reality
More than 300 episodes
Thousands of stories, fictions and documentaries
From love till death, it had everything.
Everything I couldn't in reality.
(Netflix)

Chapter15

After the never ending long lectures
We found our way to the canteen
It was a breezy afternoon
The smell of the coffee shook our bodies,
Light music to ears.
Two coffees with less sugar
The bitterness in the tip of our tongue
Wanting more.
Our first bitter-sweet love story!
(Coffee & Me)

Chapter16

When I was a kid, I thought the world was covered by a big cotton candy,
I always wanted to taste it, sometimes it looked blue, many times it looked pink and violet.
The curiosity swept in. What does it taste like?
Strawberries? Blueberries? Orange?
The closer I went I realized it wasn't cotton candy,
It was fog, that can never be held by anyone.
Like the sky, was my love
The closer I went I realized you weren't the cotton candy
You were the fog I could never hold.

Chapter17

It was five in the evening
The drizzling of rain after the scorching heat
The smell of sand, so familiar
Like a mother's touch.
The droplets of water in my face
The heat from my body is released,
The stress, the deadlines everything fades away
As a vapor, into the sky
The body can feel the cold running through the veins
I let myself drench in the rain
Hoping it would wash away my worries and sins

Chapter18

He was the sun, I was the sky
I was nothing but a vast blue sky
He painted me with colors
He made me pretty with his glowing rays
He gave me all I had
The pain, The love, The beauty
From sunrise to sunset
He gave me everything

Chapter19

The leaves started to fall,
The dried brown leaves turned into our red carpet.
The tree looked lonely without the leaves
The new fresh leaves started to grow
The trees that give us shadow, had a change
The change of new leaves
Change was the constant thing,
Yet it gave space for the new beginnings.

Chapter20

After the long hours,
We both found a seat at the bus
We plugged in our earphones
We started to play the love songs
Slowly, we started to talk about our life
That's when i realised you are the one
The best friend who is going to be there,
In the darkest nights and boring mornings
Through the long lecture hours and happy little moments.
We started to share our seat in the bus
To the desk in our class

Chapter21

The beautiful sound of water waves
Kids throwing stones into water
The ripples that created a quick vibration
The sound of the siren resonated across the harbour
People selling food at each corner
The smell of potato wedges and roasted corn
The different colored balloons
The sea shells across the beach
The collection i made
That remains in my hand
(Day at the beach)

Chapter22

I look up to you every time and everyday
Up above you is gleamingly shine
You glow in the dark like his eyes
Maybe you too were born, from the same lord's heart
Even when you are surrounded by ten million stars.
You are the only one that can be seen by my naked eyes.
As if every star around you is a sprinkle of dust.
You change your looks each day.
You diminish and grow just like my hope
But still never away you move
You make us peaceful with your cozy light
Which makes us sleep tight.

Chapter23

You are everywhere, every time
In my brighter days and weaker nights
Sometimes i see you, sometimes i don't
You follow me, like a secret admirer
You hold the sun high, to show us light
You hold the moon high, to give us pretty nights
You are nothing, but just everything
You change colors, just like the moods of evening
You are the mirror, of my heart
What i see when i see you, is nothing but me
You give a beautiful rainbow after the storm
I give a beautiful poem after the pain

Chapter24

The stars are my love
The moon is my home
The sky is my everything
Forevermore.

Chapter25

I was scrolling through Instagram
I saw his art for the first time
I was never a big fan of art,
Until i saw his, it had life in it
It had reality, the pain, the hurt, the love
That's when i fell in love,
With the art and the artist.

Chapter26

Late night chats
Our inside jokes and deep talks
His sarcasm and my stickers
I talked and he listened
He talked and i listened
It was a perfect give and take
We never expected anything from each other
We kept loving each other.

Chapter27

Love travels through the infinite galaxies,
The heart wanders into the love to get lost
Lost in you, the definition of love
Love is something i could feel by calling your name
Love is something i could tell by seeing your face
Through the earth, moon, stars and galaxies my love remains the same

Love is you.
Love is me.

Chapter28

Happy moments? Euphoric moments?
It's never gonna last
Same goes for the bad and sad moments
It's never gonna last forever either
We laugh, we smile, we cry
We go through everything because life gets boring if it's in the same phase
We push harder, we rest
We support, we lean on each other's shoulder
It's all about the balance
The balance between love and hate
The balance between sweet and sour
Life is the sweetest,
With some sour bites which indeed makes the sweet sweeter.

Chapter29

I was bored at night,
"Want to sing together" he asked
"I would love to" I said
(That's when i fell for him)

Chapter30

It was my birthday.
0 calls, 0 texts.
They forgot. With tears in my eyes'
I took my cycle, went to my favourite bakery
Sat in the right side corner, near the window
I ordered a chocolate mundt cake
I stared outside the window, i could see the people.
I could see the vehicles passing by
The noise cancelled out, i could hear some muffled voices
I find myself holding the chocolate cake
I took a bite, it was filled with chocolate syrup, Nutella and some crunchy nuts
It was moist and soft
With every bite a tear dropped
I continue to eat alone.

Chapter31

I was confused
Should I look at the stars above?
Or the brightest star sitting next to me?
(It was you all along)

Chapter32

She stood by through the pain
She held me when I cried
She loved me through all
We laughed together
We cried together.

Chapter33

I will spend my life showing how much i love you
I will spend every day to make you feel loved
I will show the world to you
You deserve nothing but the best of me
I got lucky in the department of love
You got unlimited supply of laughter and love
From me to you
Only you

Chapter34

The moment i held your hand
Everything around me stopped
The air, the wind, the motion of everything around us
All i could ever see was your eyes
And all i could ever feel was your warmth.

Chapter35

You are black
I am white
We create the hue and intensity of colors
We are the origin of colors
Without you I am nothing but a pale color
When we start to mingle
We are the lights and shadows
We exist to unite and create

Chapter36

When I look at the mirror
I see me and I see you
You are nothing but a fraction of me
The fraction that's found,
Once in a lifetime.

Chapter37

When I think about you
My words just start to arrange themselves into beautiful words.

Chapter38

You hold my heart closest to yours
I would never change a single moment
We can be a different person to every single person
But I chose to be real, the real vulnerable yet strong
Sometimes harsh but sweetest
To love you with all. And get excess from the lord to love you,
Because you are the one who deserves it.
Until I met you, I was nothing but a stranger
Roaming in the forest.
I have been searching for you all along.

Chapter39

In life there are passing clouds
But his life was a passing cloud
Everything and everyone were a variable
But in between those variables
He found his constant
He didn't realise it was her
He hasn't realised it yet,
But the undeniable love between them
Keep them closer to their heart.

Chapter40

The tall skyscrapers
The clean roads
Smell of books, coffee shops
Couples holding hands
The metro station, planetarium
The pinch of sweet in every food
The trees that give fresh air,
The orange street lights.
That's when i feel in love with the city.
(Bangalore)

Chapter41

When you left me,
You took some fragments of me
That can never be found.
(You are the missing piece)

Chapter42

You promised to hold my hand in the storm
You promised to create a forever
You held my hands making my heart flutter
We walked all morning without a reason,
Just to spend time with each other
You love me deep from your heart
But not as much as i did.

Chapter43

The little moments,
Silly jokes during class
Eating comfort food
Watching my favourite movie
Wearing a new dress
Travelling to a cold, breezy place
Enjoying a scoop of ice cream
I started to live for these moments.

Chapter44

He thought she was his everything
She left him without warning,
He was broken unable to find a way
He was confused with all the pieces
That was left behind.
She was healing herself, that's when she found him
The mirror image of her
She wanted to mend his soul
Not just mend his soul, but to give him her's
She wanted to give him everything
But with nothing in return.

Chapter45

I was broken into pieces like a broken bowl
That's when I met you, you were the golden glue that fixed my pieces together,
You didn't just fix me; you gave me the new glow I never had.
The glow that makes even the sun look smaller.
It's because of you the pieces of the puzzle make sense.
Amongst all these people something about you caught my eye
Your eyes? Your face? No. Just you! You in general.
The way you talk. The way you make things seem easier….
It's what I live for,
Knowing that you would be by my side makes it easier.

Chapter46

If I let go, the connection fades
I have nothing but memories to hold on
His presence, voice, his touch
Everything seems distant
We don't have a picture to look back
All I have is his sunshine face,
Tattooed on my brain, if I let go
It might fade away, not today.
But forever, my love is you
When you fade away so does my love.
I can't live with that.

Chapter47

Window seats, favourite music
Cool Breeze running through my hair
Going to a place without a destiny
Random snacks on the way,
A coffee break once in a while
Aesthetic pics of sky
Long waiting in the signal
Looking at those cool cars, bikes
A day in my vacation life.

Chapter48

I am the repulsion
Of all the love.
For every action there is an equal and opposite reaction,
But in love there is never equal
Just the opposite reaction.

Chapter49

Nothing rings a bell anymore,
No butterflies, no heart fluttering moments
No one makes me want to live or love
The purpose is futile
The existence is brutal.

Chapter50

When your lips met mine,
Two worlds met.
They travelled millions of miles
To get together.
Things started to look different
The colourless day had a color in it
The pain started to fade
The love started to grow.

Chapter51

You are my

Past, present and future.

Chapter52

The world exists, not like before
Your presence is diminishing
Within the earth lies hell
The place filled with your memories and reminders turned into agony
It's all nothing but ashes of my heart
Everything turned into a blur image
Truly questioning my existence

Chapter53

It was a holiday
I lied in my bed for hours
Listening to music, watching movies
Making a conversation with alexa
Living life by doing nothing
It made me happy.

Chapter54

I still hope for love
If I stop hoping
I have nothing to live for

Chapter55

"Will you be my valentine?" He asked

"But it's April." She said

"Not my valentine for a day, but my valentine for the rest of my life" he said

Chapter56

You called me, "love"
You told me "love you"
Did you mean any of it?
Did you mean some of it?
Am i the one who always blindly trusts?
Am i the only one who blindly falls?
This time I fell harder than before
I broke my heart with my own fantasies
I went from stronger to vulnerable,
Vulnerable for your love, only your love.
Everyday i wish to be loved while i sleep
And yet i drown in the fantasies of "you & I"
I sleep like a snob, to escape the reality
The reality of a life without you
And to meet the fantasy of you.

Chapter57

The heart aches to tell you how I feel,
The eyes look at you and make me kneel
The skin refreshes with your touch
The mesmerizing voice passes through my ears
Through all the senses, I feel the love
The senses grow deeper, stronger, narrower.

Chapter58

I wish i could hold your hand and apologize
I wish i could cry and beg for a second chance,
I wish i could take back what i did
I wish there was more bind and trust between us
I wish you were here with me
To my human dairy, I loved you and i always will today, tomorrow, forever
I felt this before, but not with you
You are more than something i deserve
Every time it was "i don't deserve you" to me
But this time for real, "i don't deserve you"
Now i know what that means
You were the right person and i was the wrong time
Wherever you are i will wish for your happiness
But oh darling, please forgive me for the sins i did but i never intended to
You are more than i could ever ask for.

Chapter59

It lasted the whole summer,
He was with me for one summer
It doesn't matter if it was a month or year
All that mattered is we loved each other
The four months made me want to,
Love him for nine lives
To be born again and again to be loved by him.
Our love was like ice cream
I never wanted it to melt
But in the end it did.

Chapter60

Him and I
Sky and rain
Lock and key
Light and bright
Sweet and sour
Black and white
The unbreakable bond
Bond that's visible to naked eyes
The truth is his eyes, I see myself
In his god eyes'.
We are like a pair of socks, without one another
We are nothing but a lost piece.

Chapter61

The world is the same
Everyone wants the pretty girl
The girl who dresses like a model
The girl who has a pretty smile and beautiful eyes
But no one tried to dig deep into her heart
All they wanted was her beauty
The beauty that's mesmerizing to the eyes
But they failed to acknowledge
The kind souls, the helping people
The loving people. The world doesn't deserve it,
The love and care of those kind people
The world needs "beauty standardized" girls.
But I could never be her
And I never will.

Chapter62

In a room full of crowded people, I was the least interesting, least popular
Yet you chose, the least wanted
And made me most wanted in your life.
I was the alphabet, you made me into words
Creating a meaning to my life and people in it.
I was the land and you were the water,
The gorgeous water that turned the land into a beautiful ocean.
Before you I existed,
During you I lived,
After you I tried.

Chapter63

There are three hundred unsent letters
Three thousand unsent texts,
There are moments when I stare at your contact,
I saved you on my phone, But i couldn't save you in life
I wanted to call you and tell "I still love you, always have, always will"
But I am blocked everywhere,
The places where it used to be "Good morning" "Good night" "I love you babe" "How was your day?"
It's filled with nothing but a void now.
I stare at the screen, our chats. Looking back into the memories.
It's been three years, yet everyday I wake up
Hoping you would miss me like I did.
(Wish I could tell you)

Chapter64

There are days when i want to hold your hand
There are days when i just wanna know you are there
Nothing but, your presence. Hearing your voice, just listening to songs together
With my head on your shoulder
There are no big moments or heart fluttering things.
Just you and me in the park bench
Wondering where our life is taking us!
I will love you through all the butterfly and non-butterfly moments.

Chapter65

You saved me from those pain
You loved me through the pain
The reason for my smile is you
The reason for the light is you
Within the darkness you emerged
As the saviour of my world

Chapter66

It was her all along,
Those smiles, laughter, care was her's
You looked at her the way i looked at you
The more you were distant, the harder it felt.
To see you play with her hair, to love her.
It felt like breaking my heart into millions
The way it couldn't be fixed
You sang with her, you drew beautiful memories with her.
You drew those in the white blank sheet, it was visible to the entire world
At those moments i lost myself.
Into the deep drowning darkness
But this time you weren't there,
To save me anymore.

Chapter67

My presence doesn't change the aspects of the world,
My heart gets tired because of the world
The love that's excess to this world
To live in a world that doesn't get mad,
Without my presence is the glitch in the matrix
To be present but futile in existence
To be liked but not loved
Is the real existential crisis.

Chapter68

You left me with a part of you,
The pieces don't make sense anymore
The world moved on, while i was stuck
With the pieces of you,
That couldn't fit anymore
Love existed, it binds us
It's slowly starting to fade away into the past.
It's hard to hold on anymore
I can't love because, you were the love inside me.
The origin of the everlasting feeling, I was left in the middle
Love, nevermore

Chapter69

To hold your heart, through the deepest darkest days
To hold your heart, through the brightest warmest days
Love to my heart is the drop of your love,
Love to the ocean is the drops of rain,
To hold it together and form the ocean of love.
To hold your pain and make it vein
To give you love that makes you sane.
Make you laugh behind the pain
To see that face behind the dark
To feel that love beneath the mask
Because you deserve the love of my heart.

Chapter70

You are the sun for my moon.
Without the sun, the moon is nothing but a dark space of matter.
Everything has a beginning and end,
You were the beginning and end,
But in the middle was your love.
That made sense to the beginning and made me live till the end.
Everything has a origin, you are the origin
Of my love, my words, my faith and my trust
Oh darling it's who you I write for.

Chapter71

It's been 3 months
He moved to London for a business
His flight is arriving tomorrow
I miss him a lot
Tears filled my eyes with his memories
The doorbell rang.
I opened the door
There he was with his suitcase
"Surprise" he said
I hopped on to him and started sobbing
He pulled me back and kissed me passionately
The kiss shouted "I FUCKING MISSED YOU"

Chapter72

The moment our bodies collided
The heart connected to give sparks
I buried my face in your chest
In that minute everything vanished,
The pain, the problems, the worry.
Healing the scars, that's visible to the naked eyes'
The heart flutters with the joy of being embraced
To feel protected, loved, wanted
To be collided into each other's body, to create a single soul
That's bound to eternity.

Chapter73

The smile on people's faces
The love of people's heart
The sound of birds
The drizzling of rain
The laughter of people
The smell of coffee
The small moments in my life remind me of you,
Because without you i would have never noticed the beauty of people's smiles and drizzling of rain
You are the ray of sunshine in my life
Which brightens the day and makes it better.

Chapter74

It's you and me against the world
We both are like North and South
Seems closer, but the most distant
The distance may seem distant
Unlike our love that's filled with constance.
We live in the hope of "at least we live under the same sky!"
It makes our love last eternal, to know our love existed
But to be forbidden because it's beyond the treasures in the world.

Chapter75

Sometimes i just wish i had someone to hold my hands,
Hug me tightly and just whisper " everything is going to be okay"
I want someone to hold me tightly and tell me "i love you, today, tomorrow, forever" just for the way i am
Days pass and this is the only thought that spreads harder everyday
To cuddle on cozy and winter nights
To get unlimited supply of forehead kisses
And to call me by my name the way i want to hold him closer and kiss him...
To hold hands and go for a walk every single night, talk about silly gossips
To Laugh, cry, love.
To spend evenings watching Netflix all day under one blanket
That's all i would ever ask for.

Chapter76

I want to hold your hands and dance under the mild orange street lights,

I want to play "perfect" and fall between your arms

Slowly dance along to your movements and wonder what I did to deserve you?

I want you to carry more than just my secrets , i want you to carry my love.

I am dancing with you between my arms

The breeze through your hair which makes you so handsome, that i doubt myself ...do i deserve this? Darling you look so perfect tonight

We walked through the street laughing and singing, i never realised this is all i asked for.

The cool breeze that froze my whole body, suddenly becomes warm when you hold my hand. My heart becomes warm.

I want to hold on to your embrace forever, because oh darling your touch makes me so warm.

When i hold your hand, i don't see anybody but you, just you.

Chapter77

Deep pain through the nerves
Harder it seems to get what you deserve,
To be surrounded by hundreds and welcomed by none,
Throughout the journey of life it doesn't get better
To be present but not welcomed
To be loved but not cherished

Chapter78

In this world of different kinds of people
I am glad i found you, the positive one
The happy one, the lovely one.
Itsy because you I smile everyday
I feel like i matter to someone in this world
It's all because of you
Not everyone can be remembered and loved
But you damn sure can be remembered by me forever
Because you are the magic of my life
Healer of my life
Thank you for everything, i will give you my all. Always & forever

Chapter79

After I saw you,
I stopped looking at those boys in the hallway
I stopped caring about the comments of the random guy,
I stopped thinking about the people who left me
I started to think about what it's like to be with you?
I started thinking what it takes to be with you?
When they said " i don't deserve you"
You said " Girl you are the only thing i deserve more"
That made me rip the world apart and make a throne out of gold and diamonds
With every minute that passed by the love started to go deep into the horizons
As the sun, moon and star which seems close yet thousands of miles apart from us,
My love and your love seemed to be close but yet thousands of miles apart.

Chapter80

Memories? Reminders?
Both are the same, it is painful and hurtful and connected to each other .
When i crossed the path we walked, i saw the young you and me we were so in love.
I wanted to shout "he is gonna break your heart"
"He is gonna break your heart"
But i couldn't, because i knew that i would never even listen to myself,
Because i was so in love, with who you are
And with who i am, when i am with you
The memories of you are just a reminder to not fall in love,
Ever again. Because, this heart can't take one more break.
It's already broken into million pieces
It cannot be broken far more,
The pain is inevitable.

Chapter81

I wish I could tell you how much i love you
"When i close my eyes , i see you.
When i open my eyes i long to see you.
When you are not around, i feel your presence all around me.
Every second , every minute, all time
My eyes only search for you my dear.
Call it love , madness or just my feelings
It's all the same to me.
Many have loved before. But my life stands apart from all of them because they do not have you
I can never forget you and i don't want to forget you
I will love you forever and even after that .
Truly"

Chapter82

Chapter83

Just like the light , they started to fade
Faraway where no star or moon can reach
Leaving me alone in the darkness of life
Which made it hard to survive,
In the loneliness that's vast as the skies.

Chapter84

There are days when I want to hold your hand
There are days when I just want to know you are there
Nothing but, your presence. Hearing your voice, just listening to songs together
With my head on your shoulder
There are no big moments or heart fluttering things.
Just you and me in the park bench
Wondering where our life is taking us!

Chapter85

You saved me from those pain
You loved me through the pain
The reason for my smile is you
The reason for the light is you
Within the darkness you emerged
As the saviour of my world.

Chapter86

There you were in the chaos between the physical and mental pain,
Through the darkness you found the light of love and friendship,
That travels above and beyond the horizons
For you, only for you.
The pain is gonna last for a few hours which feels like forever,
Then the after effects of the pain, the glow stays forever in your heart.
Day by day, little bit more you grow through my heart.
Just in case you need to know, you make me want to live again.

Chapter87

Our memories didn't make me happy anymore,
It started to haunt me, I couldn't sleep or eat
My heart wanted closure; my brain wanted to be closer
To you and your memories even when it hurt
That's when I knew I had to let go, of the fading memories
My heart's staying in the same memories
The more I try to let go, the more I hold on to it
Because you were the beginning
When I wanted to be your middle and end
I was your beginning, but only the beginning
When I wanted it to end with us.

Chapter88

The smile on people's faces
The love of people's heart
The sound of birds
The drizzling of rain
The laughter of people
The smell of coffee
The small moments in my life remind me of you,
Because without you I would have never noticed the beauty of people's smiles and drizzling of rain
You are the ray of sunshine in my life
Which brightens the day and makes it better.

Chapter89

I was invisible to those people's eyes'

I was visible to your beautiful eyes'

There are plenty of stars in the sky, they all look the same, except the biggest in the sky (the moon)

Which is you, to me. The brightest star in my sky.

Through the galaxies that's filled with stars

I found the prettiest star, the star even the milky way is jealous of

Even the collection of stars is nothing but just dust compared to you.

Chapter90

I wake up in the morning hoping you would be next to me

I walk through the streets hoping I would see you

I go to places thinking I might run into you randomly, then I would fall on my knees and beg you to take me back

I go to our school hoping you would be staring at the desks where we sat, like I did

Look at the place we both used to be never knowing how much we meant to each other

The corridor where I talked to you for the first time

When the ray of sunshine kissed your cheeks and the smile that was brighter than sunshine

The shy guy, the tall guy who I always admired

The guy who spoke through art, the guy who loved making others happy

The guy who I always wanted to be loved by

I can't explain it but I keep thinking about you, you feel like home. More than home. You feel like the touch of mom, the love of father, the bond of relatives, fun of friends.

Chapter91

He saw the world with love and care
He gave his all to make it gleam
He thought the world is filled with angles
That's when he saw the devil
The devil tried to take over his soul
He wore a mask to hide it all
She entered overthrowing his pain
She saw him beneath the mask
The purest soul with kindest heart
Who deserves it all.
The pure hearted saviour he is,
Their souls are connected through the pain,
Making them heal each other.

Chapter92

You make me want to look beyond the stars
You make me want to fly above the sky.
Even among the thousand stars the moon stands different
Just like the moon, you are different from every other human I have ever met.
Nobody shines like you do
Nobody makes me happy like you do.

Chapter93

We think about someone the whole day,
They run through our mind without a break
Day and night, when you eat and sleep
Even when you laugh and smile
There is a part of you always thinking about someone
And they have no idea.

Chapter94

People want to keep it casual
Move on from one person to another
After the magic faded
Is this the society i live in?
Where did the genuine love go?
Holding on to each other's hand
Until they both can't walk
Feeding each other during busy days
Morning coffee and forehead kisses
A long walk with complete silence
Admiring their flaws and imperfections
Where did it all go?
Everyone needs a change
No one wants to stay in close range.

Chapter95

What is love?
Even when the world's against you,
You stand for each other
You let your ego down and apologize
Because you can never be without each other
You endure any kind of pain
Just to spend the rest of your life with each other.

Chapter96

He tattooed her eyes' in his chest
He was distant from her
He wanted to look at her everyday
Every hour, every minute, every second
The rules of the world were against
He carried her eyes in his heart
He treasured her more than gold and diamonds
He loved her with every cell in his body

Chapter97

We give people plenty of chances
But do we give ourselves a chance?
We blame, we stress, we never rest
When is it that we start hoping on ourselves?
(Hope on you)

Chapter98

Life is like a spider's web
We built it so many times and yet it gets destroyed, but we never give up
We built our web of life again and again
Even in our strengths and weaknesses we never quit,
We rest and come back stronger
That's the cycle of life, to try again and again.

Chapter99

When i look at the stars
It looks like he is watching me
From far away,
That's why i live. To live my life
And his.
To do all those things he wanted to
To make his soul rest in peace.

Chapter100

Everything was going fine
Until one day, he disappeared
Not only from my life. From this world
Yesterday he was my everything
Today he is nothing but another dead person,
People will mourn today, tomorrow,
They just move on after a while
While i am here stuck with his memories
Forever and beyond .

Chapter101

"What do I give in return for your love?" He asked
"I need nothing but you" she said
His soothing presence, His humor, His positivity
Is all she needed, Until the end.

Chapter102

The universe takes away something
To give something even bigger, greater and stronger.
I never believed in all of it
Until I met him, I thought I would never laugh again,
Never love again. But then he came
Creating the sparks again in my dead heart.
A rebirth of my hope.

Chapter103

I used to listen to everyone's talk
I stay up late at night for my best friend to talk about her life
I stay up an hour late at school to console a girl.
I listen to my mom's spiritual talks,
But when he came, I listened
But for a change, he listened to me too
That's when I knew I have never talked about me
It felt like I was leaning on his chest
Wrapping my arms around him,
It felt like a soothing love song.

Chapter104

You came into my life from nowhere
But you made my life so fair
The small moments are what I live for,
The laughs, the smiles, the small heart beats
Stuck between your cute smile that makes my heart run miles.

Chapter105

He kissed her forehead
"Good morning, sunshine" he said
His sleepy face, sunlight kissing his cheeks
She never wanted to wake up
From this beautiful dream

Chapter106

Love isn't easy,
It's dumb luck
Some get everything
Some get nothing.
Isn't the whole point of life,
To be needed by someone?
To feel welcomed into someone's arms
Is one in a billion possibility

Chapter107

To hold your heart, through the deepest darkest days
To hold your heart, through the brightest warmest days
Love to my heart is the drop of your love,
Love to the ocean is the drops of rain,
To hold it together and form the ocean of love.
To hold your pain and make it vein
To give you love that makes you sane.
Make you laugh behind the pain
To see that face behind the dark
To feel that love beneath the mask
Because you deserve the love of my heart.

Chapter108

He was the sun, I was the sky
I was nothing but a vast blue sky
He painted me with colors
He made me pretty with his glowing rays
He gave me all I had
The pain, The love, The beauty
From sunrise to sunset
He gave me everything.

Chapter109

We both were waiting for the bus to arrive
Under the shades of the tree
The dry leaves gave an aesthetic feel
We stood in a corner staring at all the bus
Waiting for ours to arrive.
Slowly we started talking from strangers,
We became friends.
The unexpected bond became something I looked forward to.

Chapter110

It was a sunday morning
I woke up and he was not in bed
I found him in the kitchen
Preparing all of my favourite dishes
He didn't notice me, I watched him cook
It was the cutest moment
I hugged him from behind, giving all my warmth
"How did I get so lucky?" I whispered
"Not more than me" He whispered

Chapter111

I love him knowing we can never be together
I spend time with him as if it's our last minute
Because the future is unsure
But I wanna spend the rest of my life
Knowing I gave him everything i can
Because he was the right person
And I was the wrong time.

Chapter112

The world around me was drowning
The harder it seemed to take breathes
Things around me turned into a black hole
When I was about to lose myself
He saw me through the wall,
The wall of insecurities
He entered the world of calamities
To rebuild my world with love and care
I love you till big bang,
I love you till big bang
He healed me once and for all.

Chapter113

We are like left and right eye
Closest to each other but,
Can never be together
We seem closest yet far away.

Chapter114

I saw myself in your eyes
I fell in love, why do I love you like this?
Why am I breathing your love?
Oh darling, you are enough to live a thousand years

It ends with me.

9 798889 752547

Printed by Libri Plureos GmbH in Hamburg,
Germany